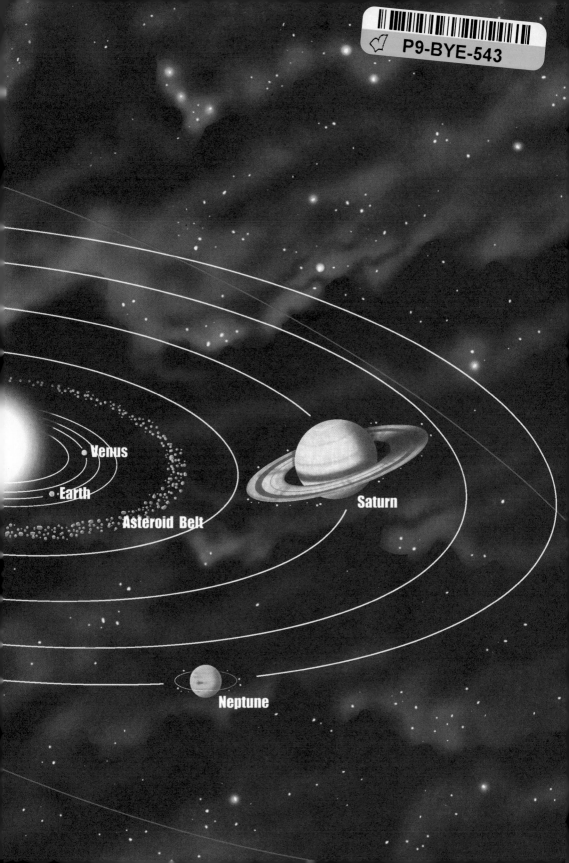

If an Asteroid Hit

Earth

If an Asteroid Hit

Earth

Ray Spangenburg and Kit Moser

Franklin Watts

A DIVISION OF GROLIER PUBLISHING
NEW YORK · LONDON · HONG KONG · SYDNEY
DANBURY, CONNECTICUT

To

PAT AND JOHN
*for encouragement and conversation
and for being there always*

Photographs ©: AP/Wide World Photos: 80 (AP Newsfeatures Photo); Archive Photos: 43; Finley Holiday Film: 63; Gary Ladd: 14; Liaison Agency, Inc.: 48 (Roy Gumpel); Lunar and Planetary Institute: 29; NASA: 30 (Hubble Space Telescope Comet Team), 23, 28, 51 bottom, 66, 67, 74, 77, 85, 96, 109; National Museum of Natural History, Smithsonian Institution: 70 right; Photo Researchers: 44, 45 (Lynette Cook/SPL), 12, 92 (John Foster), 16 (François Gohier), 50, 110 (David A. Hardy/SPL), 68 (Seth Joel/SPL), 34, 35 (Calvin Larsen), 64, 100 (NASA/SPL), 17, 18, 19 (David Parker/SPL), 70 left (Pekka Parviainen/SPL), 2, 58, 76, 104, 106 (SPL), 61, 103 (Joe Tucciarone/SPL), 51 top (US Geological Survey/SPL), cover, 8, 20 (D. Van Ravenswaay/SPL), 89 (Erik Viktor/SPL); Photofest: 87 (ILM), 57; Stocktrek: 38.

**Visit Franklin Watts on the Internet at:
http://publishing.grolier.com**

Library of Congress Cataloging-in-Publication Data

Spangenburg, Ray, 1939–
    If an asteroid hit Earth / by Ray Spangenburg and Kit Moser.
       p.   cm.—(Out of this world)
    Includes bibliographical references and index.
    Summary: Examines the origins of asteroids, their effects on hitting Earth in the past and present, and many of the asteroids in the solar system.
    ISBN 0-531-11716-2 (lib. bdg.)   0-531-16512-4 (pbk.)
    1. Asteroids—Collisions with Earth Juvenile literature. 2. Catastrophes (Geology) Juvenile literature. [1. Asteroids.] I. Moser, Diane, 1944– . II. Title. III. Series: Out of this world (Franklin Watts, Inc.)
QB377.S63   2000
523.44—dc21   99-32247

GROLIER
PUBLISHING   1 2 3 4 5 6 7 8 9 10 R 09 08 07 06 05 04 03 02 01 00

Acknowledgments

The best books are the products of many minds and many conversations. The knowledge, expertise, and resources of many people flow into the words on the page, and we would especially like to thank some of the many people who have contributed to *If an Asteroid Hit Earth*.

First of all, a special appreciation to Sam Storch, Lecturer at the American Museum-Hayden Planetarium, who reviewed the manuscript and made many insightful suggestions. Also a special thanks goes to our editor at Franklin Watts, Melissa Stewart, whose steady flow of enthusiasm, creativity, energy, and clippings of late-breaking news have infused this series.

To Tony Reichhardt and John Rhea, once our editors at the former *Space World Magazine*, thank you for starting us out on the fascinating journey we have taken during our years of writing about space.

Contents

An artist's representation of a huge asteroid striking Earth.

Killer Space Rock

I't's Anytown, USA. People get up with the morning sun and go to work and school. They drive their cars and trucks down freeways and turnpikes. No one has noticed the huge, dark killer rock that is hurtling undetected through space at that very moment, headed straight for the blue waters of planet Earth.

Suddenly, the daytime sky fills with blinding light as an *asteroid* plunges through the atmosphere. People along the Atlantic Coast shudder at the distant roar. What is it? The sound becomes steadily louder and more piercing. Seconds later, a rock the size of a house slams into the water a few hundred miles off the coast and plunges to the ocean floor. Its intense, fiery heat kills thousands of sea creatures. The force of the impact sends out giant waves in every direction.

Within minutes, *tsunamis*—fast-moving ocean waves that retain their destructive energy while traveling huge distances—pound the coast relentlessly, striking again and again. A giant wall of water crashes through houses and businesses, crushes cars, tears up trees, and churns objects, animals, and people. What is not submerged and drowned is crushed and scoured by the crashing, roiling waters. Floods cover the land for miles inland, and where busy towns and cities once prospered, now only piles of rubble remain.

Chapter 1

A Real-Life Asteroid Attack

O f course, the scene described in the prologue is imaginary. Could it happen, though? Yes, it could. In fact, something like it has happened several times in the past. By a stroke of luck, nothing so big has hit Earth since human beings have been around. However, scientists have plenty of evidence suggesting that asteroids have bombarded Earth in the past. The giant space rocks have never destroyed great cities, but they have gouged great holes in early Earth's crust. They have also wiped out many ancient species, including the lordly dinosaurs.

At one time, dinosaurs ruled the world. They roamed Earth's surface for 160 million years.* You know many of their names—

---

* Human beings have been around for a much shorter time—only 200,000 years, a tiny blip in the history of our planet.

An asteroid probably ended the reign of the dinosaurs.

Tyrannosaurus, Allosaurus, and *Velociraptor*—and you have probably seen them in movies such as *Jurassic Park.* You have definitely seen some of their descendants, which include alligators and crocodiles, turtles, and 10,000 species of birds. But aside from these relatively puny leftovers, the great dinosaurs have completely vanished.

For a long time no one was sure exactly why the dinosaurs disappeared. It was one of the great mysteries of our planet's past. Then, in the early 1980s, Nobel Prize-winning physicist Luis Alvarez and his son, geologist Walter Alvarez, came up with the answer.

About 65 million years ago, the whole world turned into a fiery nightmare. A huge rock the size of a small town came hurtling out of the sky, flaming and thundering through the atmosphere. As it approached Earth's surface, it became a raging, roaring fireball. Then, with a giant explosion, it plunged into the planet's crust. The ground trembled, and the oceans swelled into giant tidal waves. Fire raged everywhere, and the sky blackened with smoke, ash, and dust. The huge, dark cloud filled the skies worldwide and blotted out the warmth and light of the Sun for many months.

Within a few weeks of the asteroid impact, the lack of sunlight caused plants to die. Then, animals that depended on the plants for food began to starve, and soon animals that ate the plant-eaters found less and less to eat too. The food chain disintegrated. Scientists estimate that 90 percent of all organisms living on Earth at that time became extinct within about 100 years.

The Road to Discovery

How did Luis and Walter Alvarez come up with this scenario? In 1980, the two men were examining some ancient *sediment.* Like all geologists, Walter was accustomed to analyzing the layers of sediment that

In this photograph of the Grand Canyon, it is easy to identify four separate layers of sediment.

nature has laid down age after age like a pile of papers on a messy desk. He knew that, for the most part, the sediment layers on the bottom were laid down earlier than the ones near the top. Although layers of sediment are laid down one on top of the other, the lower layers sometimes rise to the surface and become exposed as Earth's *crust* erodes and shifts. Despite this movement, geologists know how to read Earth's layers like the pages in a history book.

The sediment the Alvarezes were looking at came from a thin layer that was 65 million years old. It was sandwiched like a piece of lunch meat between two much larger layers. The bottom of this "sandwich" was a layer of rock laid down during the Cretaceous period, when dinosaurs last walked on Earth. The top of the sandwich consisted of a more recent layer that formed during the Tertiary period, which followed the Cretaceous period.

Walter Alvarez knew that when scientists from different parts of the world looked at these two large layers, they found lots of dinosaur fossils in the bottom layer, but none in the top layer. Geologists had long suspected that the thin layer might contain some clues about what happened to the dinosaurs.

Because this thin layer separates the Cretaceous and Tertiary periods, it has come to be called the "K/T boundary" (K for Cretaceous [after the German spelling] and T for Tertiary). Wherever this particular layer of sediment is preserved, it looks exactly the same. It is a thin, distinctive layer of gray clay. The chemical elements in this layer are nearly identical throughout the world. It's also about the same thickness everywhere—only a little thicker in Mexico and the Caribbean Sea. From this evidence, scientists concluded that a single monumental event affected the entire planet and lasted a very short time—probably about 1 year.

The thin K/T layer of clay shown in this photo suggests that an asteroid collided with Earth about 65 million years ago.

What caused this enormous change? Many theories existed, but no one knew the real answer for sure.

Luis Alvarez introduced methods and tools commonly used in physics to examine the material from the K/T boundary layer, and what he saw amazed him. The sediment contained an unusually high concentration of an element called iridium—a substance that is very rare on Earth, but abundant in objects in space. In fact, the relative amounts of iridium in the K/T boundary layer closely match the typical makeup of a *meteorite*, a chunk of rock from space that has fallen to the surface of a planet or moon. In the words of asteroid expert John Lewis, "Iridium is, in effect, an alien fingerprint." As the Alvarez team concluded, parts of this worldwide layer of sediment appear to have come from outer space!

This meteorite was found in Arizona.

Luis Alvarez: The "Wild Idea Man of Physics"

Some of the best scientists have a rare talent for putting apparently unrelated ideas together and coming up with new ways of looking at things. Luis Alvarez was such a scientist, and sometimes his ideas were so far out that people called him the "wild idea man of physics."

Luis Alvarez

When Luis and Walter Alvarez first proposed the idea that an asteroid about 6 miles (10 kilometers) wide had caused the death of the dinosaurs, people laughed. But father and son had combined keen observation (noticing high levels of iridium in soil from the K/T boundary), with knowledge about several fields of science (physics, geology, and chemistry), careful measurements, and intuition to come up with a theory that turned out to have a lot more going for it than most people thought.

This was by no means Luis Alvarez's first success. During World War II (1939–1945), Alvarez had worked on microwave radar research and contributed to numerous wartime applications of radar that have continued uses today, including microwave beacons and a ground-controlled landing approach system. After the war, he helped develop the first proton linear accelerator and the liquid hydrogen bubble chamber, both key instruments for studying the behavior and structure of subatomic particles. In 1968, he received the Nobel Prize in physics for his work on a group of extremely short-lived subatomic particles.

When the Alvarez team first published their results, they were greeted with skepticism. Over the following years, though, more and more evidence began to pile up, and slowly the Alvarez theory became more and more believable.

For example, in 1984, scientists found small particles of shocked, or fractured, quartz and glassy droplets mixed into the K/T layer. These clues were further evidence of a worldwide catastrophe involving high energy and extreme temperatures.

All the findings began to point in one direction: A very large object from space probably smashed into Earth 65 million years ago, possibly near the Caribbean Basin, where the K/T boundary layer is thickest and contains large, glassy droplets.

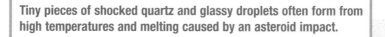

Tiny pieces of shocked quartz and glassy droplets often form from high temperatures and melting caused by an asteroid impact.

An artist's representation of what Earth might have been like after an asteroid hit 65 million years ago

Scientists began to look at a lot of "what-if" questions. They ran computer models, played out scenarios, and made calculations. Their findings were devastating. They saw that such an impact would have flung 100 trillion tons of debris at high speeds beyond Earth's atmosphere. Within an hour, the debris would have encircled Earth and re-entered the atmosphere as fireballs that scorched much of the planet's surface and burned its forests. This deluge of flaming debris could explain why the same iridium-rich clay layer appears all over the world—and why the clay contains soot.

The computer models also showed that the impact's explosion would have caused vast chemical reactions in the upper atmosphere. Acid would have rained into the oceans and rivers, leaching out toxic chemicals. Much of the air would have filled with poisonous gas. Enormous dust clouds kicked up by the blast would have blocked out the Sun for at least a year. Without sunlight, vegetation would have died, cutting off the food chain at its source. Temperatures would have dropped dramatically, putting most of the world in a deep freeze. Animals not killed by the blast, the fires, the toxic gases, and the acid rain would have died of starvation or cold.

Where Is the Crater?

By the end of the 1980s, evidence had piled up to support the idea that a gigantic object from space smashed into Earth at the end of the Age of the Dinosaurs. But, if so, where was the impact *crater*? If something that big had hit Earth, there should be a pretty big hole somewhere.

Scientists began checking *satellite* images for signs of craters. The first place they looked was on land in the Americas. Experts suspected that the strike occurred on land because the blast had produced large amounts of shocked quartz grains, and not much quartz exists on the ocean floor.

Of course, scientists knew it might be difficult to find the crater. After all, the impact had taken place 65 million years ago. Over time, erosion might have filled in the hole. Natural forces—erupting volcanoes that spill lava over the land surface, blowing winds, roaring rivers, and growing vegetation—could have changed the surface of the land at the impact site. Oceans, rivers, and lakes might have shifted, and sediment deposits might have filled in the depression.

Still, scientists reasoned, the monster crater must have originally been at least 75 miles (120 km) across, so there should be some sign of it. Unless, of course, the object happened to hit in the middle of an ocean. If so, scientists might never find the crater.

As it turned out, the first important clues to the impact crater's location had turned up long before the Alvarez team studied the tell-tale iridium in the K/T boundary layer. However, almost no one knew about these clues until more than a decade after the Alvarezes published their findings.

In 1947, a group of geologists in Mexico had done a series of tests for the Mexican oil company PEMEX. As the scientists searched for oil deposits, they found traces of an odd circular area approximately 3,300 feet (1,000 meters) underground. The site was near the town of Chicxulub, which is located on Mexico's Yucatan Peninsula. The geologists drilled a test well nearby but found no oil, so they moved on. The *core* samples they took seemed strange, though, and no one could explain why.

The Formation of a Crater

A crater forms when a small object crashes into an object that is large enough to sustain the blow without crumbling to pieces. When a meteorite hits the surface of a planet or moon, the energy of the impact breaks up material on the surface, melts it, and flings it upward. Beneath the impact, a saucer-shaped indentation, or crater, forms. Below the saucer, the rock is fractured. Pieces of debris from the impact may be propelled upward and then fall back to Earth, creating secondary craters around the main crater.

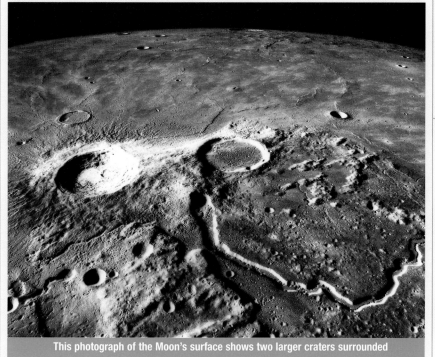

This photograph of the Moon's surface shows two larger craters surrounded by secondary craters.

In 1966, another geologist hired by PEMEX examined the same site. As he looked at the area, he realized it must be a buried crater from a major impact. Like the earlier team, he concluded that there was no oil at the site. As a result, PEMEX lost interest in the area. Because company policy prohibited the geologist from mentioning what he had seen to anyone outside the company, the buried crater remained a secret.

In 1978, geologist Glen Penfield, also a contractor for PEMEX, began a magnetic survey over the waters of the Gulf of Mexico. He too was searching for oil. In the process, Penfield found a stunning geological clue. Beneath the water was a semicircular structure with an elevated peak in the middle. Penfield knew what he was looking at—the remains of a very large impact.

Penfield talked to his colleagues at PEMEX. Some of them remembered what earlier geologists had noticed on land. Penfield compared a map he had made to maps created by the other geologists. This revealed a crater more than 62 miles (100 km) in diameter.* Penfield later recalled, "This was one of the greatest moments of my life," one of those moments scientists live for, when they piece something together that no one else has ever noticed.

When Penfield read about the Alvarezes' findings in 1980, he was sure the crater he had found was the 65-million-year-old site of the impact that killed the dinosaurs. Finally, he convinced his supervisor at PEMEX that they should present a paper at a meeting of geologists in Los Angeles. They needed to get the information out of the company files and into the scientific community. Not until 1991, though—more than a decade after the Alvarezes' discovery—did the location of the 65-million-year-old crater become widely published and generally accepted.

* Some experts think the crater originally may have been up to 186 miles (300 km) wide.

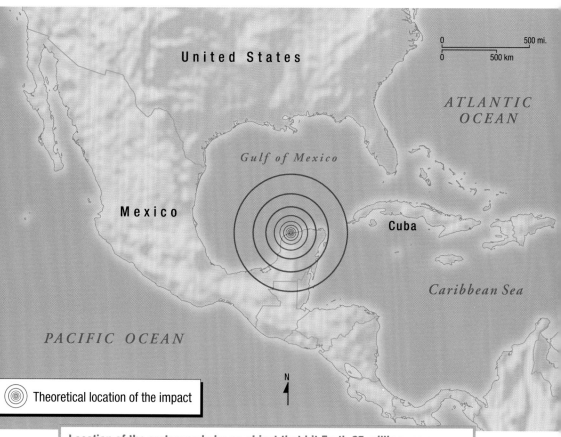

United States

ATLANTIC
OCEAN

Gulf of Mexico

Mexico

Cuba

Caribbean Sea

PACIFIC OCEAN

N

0 _____ 500 mi.
0 _____ 500 km

◎ Theoretical location of the impact

Location of the crater made by an object that hit Earth 65 million years ago

Since then, researchers in Arkansas have reported finding boulders as large as 50 feet (15 m) across that they believe were flung out of the crater on the Yucatan Peninsula. These huge rocks are now perched atop hills 250 feet (76 m) high, too high to have reached these positions in any other way, according to geologists. Just imagine how powerful the explosion must have been to throw such huge chunks of rock 1,000 miles (1,600 km).

The Dinosaur Killer: The Facts

The Object: An asteroid 6 miles (10 km) wide that traveled 40,000 miles (64,000 km) per hour and had an explosive force more than 20 million times greater than a hydrogen bomb

When: 65 million years ago

Where It Hit: Yucatan Peninsula in Mexico, near the spot where the town of Chicxulub now stands; part of the crater extends into the Gulf of Mexico

The Damage: Extinction of 90 percent of all species living on Earth, destruction of forests, months of a freezing cold "impact winter" caused by debris in the atmosphere blocking the Sun

What If? If an object of this size hit Earth today, it would certainly mean the end of civilization as we know it along with the extinction of many species, probably including human beings

The Risk: One per 50 million to 100 million years

A Fragment of the Bullet

In November 1998, scientist Frank Kyte of the University of California in Los Angeles published another intriguing piece of the K/T puzzle. He had found what he believed to be a piece of the asteroid that hammered into Earth 65 million years ago. Many scientists like to call the crater at Chicxulub the "smoking gun" of the event that caused the extinction of the dinosaurs. If so, Kyte's piece of evidence would be a fragment of the bullet.

Three years earlier, while examining a core of sediment from the K/T layer of the floor of the Pacific Ocean, Kyte came across something that caught his attention. As he sifted through the fine brown sediment, he noticed a light-colored speck that was larger than the rest. Though tiny—about the size of a match head—it was a thousand times larger than the surrounding particles. Kyte knew it was too large to have been blown by the wind. As he explained, "It had to fall from the sky to get into the sediment."

Peter Schultz, a geologist and impact expert from Brown University, has calculated that the Chicxulub asteroid approached Earth from the southeast at a 30-degree angle. If he's right, the asteroid's impact would have sent a plume of debris due west. Schultz believes that a piece of the asteroid could easily have landed in the Pacific Ocean 5,400 miles (8,690 km) away, where Kyte's core samples were taken.

When Kyte ran a chemical and microscopic analysis on the fragment, he found that it had a high iridium content—a clear indication that it came from space. Kyte's analysis also showed that the fragment was a tiny chip from an asteroid. This evidence convinced most scientists that the dinosaur killer was probably an asteroid—not a *comet*.

It's Raining Rocks and Fire

The Chicxulub asteroid is not the only giant space rock that has struck our planet. Myths, legends, and accounts from ancient civilizations include frightening stories of impact events. Some tell of stones raining down from the sky. Others describe villages and towns that were destroyed by unexplained fires from the heavens. Even the Bible, written as long ago as 1420 B.C., records in the book of Joshua that "great stones from heaven" were cast down and many people died. Accounts from China, France, England, Germany, Japan, Italy, and India date back as far as 476. These stories unquestionably recall meteorite hits and fireballs caused by chunks of asteroids and comets that plunged to Earth or exploded in midair.

Evidence of massive collisions does not end there. The Moon's craters clearly show where objects from space have struck our closest neighbor. One of these craters, named Tycho, measures 53 miles (85 km) across. It tells the story of a giant impact that occurred 100 million years ago.

An asteroid may have stripped the planet Mercury of its outer layers.

Some scientists even propose that a giant impact formed our Moon. They believe that when our planet was in its final stages of formation, a young planet about the size of Mars smashed into Earth. Some of the material from that huge collision flew off into space and became our Moon.

An ancient asteroid collision may also explain why the small planet Mercury contains very high proportions of metal. Computer simulations show that a glancing blow from a large asteroid may have blasted off most of Mercury's rocky *mantle*, leaving behind only its iron core. Our next-door neighbor, the planet Venus, may also show the results of a giant, cataclysmic impact. Venus has *retrograde* rotation. It spins in the opposite direction of all the other plants. Scientists think an ancient collision may have whipped this neighboring planet around and reversed its spin.

In 1998, scientists uncovered evidence suggesting that a huge asteroid may have struck Mars at some point in the past, releasing torrents of water that may once have been trapped beneath the planet's surface. This theory might explain why we can see giant overflow channels on Mars.

The evidence abounds. Throughout the history of our solar system, asteroids and comets have crashed violently into all the planets and moons.

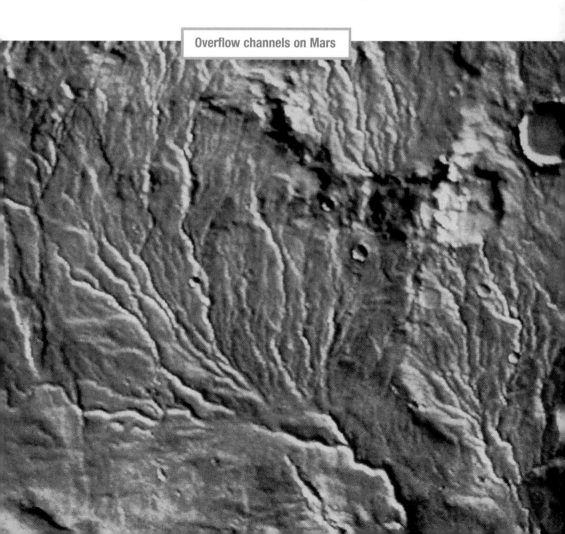

Overflow channels on Mars

Seeing Is Believing

Evidence is one thing, but seeing is believing. Our opportunity to do just that came in 1994. Astronomers on Earth had a ringside seat as the broken pieces of a renegade comet named Shoemaker-Levy 9 smashed into the hot gassy clouds of the giant planet Jupiter.

Dark red spots show where pieces of the comet Shoemaker-Levy 9 struck Jupiter in 1994.

Telescopes all over the world were trained on the event. The Hubble Space Telescope, one of NASA's orbiting observatories, also had an excellent view. The fireworks show was spectacular, but the event was also deeply sobering. Jupiter took twenty-one hits from Shoemaker-Levy 9, and each one produced a plume of fire that would have enveloped our entire planet.

Even though Shoemaker-Levy 9 hit a far-off planet, it doesn't take much imagination to realize that a similar collision could easily affect Earth. The K/T event may have taken place 65 million years ago, but the Shoemaker-Levy 9 impact took place in our own time.

In 1996, another warning came. Scientists watched with alarm as an asteroid came within 280,000 miles (451,000 km) of Earth—nearly as close as our Moon.

These events have made it clear that massive collisions are still happening in our solar system, and that asteroids sometimes come frighteningly close to Earth. In fact, experts estimate that thousands of asteroids have orbits that cross Earth's orbit, and, yes, another big one will someday crash into our planet. We don't know when. It might happen a million years from now, or it might happen next year.

Chapter 2

Traces of Earth's Violent Visitors

Despite all the evidence we now have of asteroid and comet impacts, it took a long time for people to realize that large objects from space have struck Earth several times during its 4.5-billion-year history. In 1807, a stone meteorite that fell in Connecticut was closely examined by two professors from Yale University. They announced that it had come from space. When Thomas Jefferson, who was president at the time, heard this report, he said he "would find it easier to believe that two Yankee professors would lie, than that stones should fall from the sky."

Even for intelligent people like Thomas Jefferson, fist-sized chunks of rock falling from the sky were difficult enough to accept. A cosmic impact large enough to make a huge hole in the ground was unthinkable. So, up until the twentieth century, most geologists thought that all craters on Earth were caused by volcanoes. Not until the 1890s did anyone begin to seriously consider another possibility.

The first clues came from some rocks found near a huge crater on an otherwise flat, nearly featureless plain close to Flagstaff, Arizona. The crater was 3,960 feet (1,200 m) wide and 570 feet (174 m) deep. When the rocks were examined by a Philadelphia mineral dealer named A. E. Foote, he was amazed by what he saw. He decided to travel to Arizona and see the site for himself. Foote noticed that huge segments of layered rock were tipped outward from the rim of the crater. He also found numerous iron meteorites and noted some small, black diamonds in the iron. What Foote didn't see was any evidence of volcanic activity.

Other geologists also examined the site. They were puzzled too. None of them could explain their strange findings. Most concluded that the crater was volcanic, even though they didn't know exactly how it had formed.

In 1902, a mining engineer named D. M. Barringer and a physicist and explosives expert named Benjamin C. Tilghman visited the site. The two men examined the crater carefully. They studied the deposits along the rim and drilled the crater floor for samples. Finally, they came to the conclusion that this big hole in the ground was caused by a huge meteorite made of a nickel-iron alloy. They believed that the meteorite remained buried beneath the crater floor.

Barringer (Meteor) Crater: The Facts

The Object: An iron-rich asteroid 300 feet (100 m) across

Where It Hit: The desert, near what is now Flagstaff, Arizona

When: 50,000 years ago

The Damage: A crater 3,960 feet (1,200 m) wide and 570 feet (174 m) deep

What If: If an object of the same size exploded above a modern city, the multi-megaton blast would flatten everything for miles. There would be devastating local damage, but no widespread effects. If an object of the same size exploded above the ocean, it could cause a small tsunami and flooding.

The Risk: One to ten per 100 years

Barringer Crater in Arizona was formed when an asteroid struck Earth 22,000 years ago. The building at the bottom of the photo is a research center.

Even though most geologists did not agree with this idea, Barringer set about mining the crater that is known today as Barringer Crater, or Meteor Crater. (Of course, the second name is misleading, since meteors never reach Earth's surface! Meteorite Crater or Asteroid Crater would be better names.)

Barringer never found the remains of the meteorite beneath the crater. It probably disintegrated on impact. However, Barringer did find proof that he was right about the process that formed the crater. One of his most important discoveries was a deposit of fused quartz glass—a substance that is not formed by volcanic processes. Scientists have since learned that fused quartz glass frequently forms when a large asteroid hits Earth's surface. Today Meteor Crater is recognized as one of the best known examples of an impact crater on land.

A Smashing Record: Some Asteroid Craters on Earth
Vital Statistics

Location	Approximate Age in Years	Estimated Size of Crater
BARRINGER CRATER FLAGSTAFF, ARIZONA	50,000	3,960 feet (1,200 m)
ODESSA, TEXAS	50,000	528 feet (161 m)
CHICXULUB, MEXICO	65 million	62 miles (100 km)
MJØLNIR CRATER	150 million	1.25 miles (2 km)
BARENTS SEA MANICOUAGAN, QUEBEC, CANADA	212 million	62 miles (100 km)
ACRAMAN, AUSTRALIA	570 million	99 miles (160 km)
BEAVERHEAD, MONTANA	600 million	37 miles (60 km)
SUDBURY, ONTARIO, CANADA	1.85 billion	124 miles (200 km)
VREDEFORT, SOUTH AFRICA	1.97 billion	87 miles (140 km)

The Tunguska Event

On the morning of June 30, 1908, about the time Barringer and Tilghman were examining Barringer Crater in Arizona, a stunning explosion took place in the forests of Siberia, near a village known as Tunguska. Thunderous sounds were heard as far away as St. Petersburg, Russia. A strange light was seen in the still darkened sky over Oslo, Norway. A woman in England wrote that she saw the night sky glow on the horizon at midnight and turn blue with bands of pinkish clouds. The following night, a reddish glow was still visible from much of northern Europe.

These distant signs told the story of an enormous explosion that took place deep in the central Siberian wilderness, where the only witnesses were a group of nomadic reindeer herders. No one was killed outright, although one man died later of injuries from the blast, and many reindeer were lost or killed. The herders' tents were flattened, and many of the men were thrown to the ground or knocked unconscious. Some were deafened by the roar, and all of them remembered it for the rest of their lives.

Seismic measurements recorded in England intrigued scientists, but because the area was remote—and because Russia was hovering on the edge of revolution—no one investigated the blast until 1924. At that time, a few geologists interviewed witnesses, but no one studied the site of the explosion until 1927, nearly two decades after the event. What scientists saw when they finally arrived was both chilling and amazing.

As they approached the site, the scientists observed trees charred by a fire that had enveloped the area and spread rapidly through the forest that dreadful morning in 1908. The scientists could see that, in a roughly circular region about 36 miles (60 km) across, trees had been blown flat by the blast, radiating out from the center like the spokes of a bicycle wheel. The trees at the center still stood upright, but they were stripped of their branches. It is frightening to imagine what could have happened if the asteroid had exploded over the populous city of St. Petersburg, only a few hundred miles to the west.

Trees were knocked flat and stripped bare by the Tunguska explosion of 1908.

Tunguska Explosion: The Facts

The Object: A stony asteroid 150 to 200 ft (50 to 60 m) across

Where It Hit: Exploded in midair near Tunguska, Siberia

When: 1908

The Damage: Forest trees flattened in a radius of 36 miles (60 km), widespread fire

What If: If a similar explosion occurred above a city, it would flatten buildings for miles and kill or maim residents. There would be devastating local damage, but no widespread effects. If an object of this size exploded above the ocean, a small tsunami and flooding might result.

The Risk: One to ten per 100 years

The investigators at Tunguska were puzzled by what they didn't see. There was no crater. They could find no sign of a meteorite impact. Still, they concluded that an impact by a sizable object must have caused what they saw. Was it a comet made of lightly packed material that fell apart before it hit? Or was it an asteroid that vaporized in midair above the ground?

Computer simulations performed in the 1990s helped confirm that a stony asteroid 150 to 200 feet (50 to 60 m) in diameter probably caused the great explosion. That's about half to two-thirds the size of a football field. In 1994, scientists found fragments of a stony meteorite embedded in trees at the site. Like the computer simulations, these findings provided strong evidence that the Tunguska event was caused by an asteroid or a *meteoroid* that exploded in midair before reaching Earth's surface.

Recently Discovered Craters

As scientists pieced together new clues to our planet's impact past, more discoveries sprang up. In 1998, geologists examining the high sea cliffs along the southeastern coast of Argentina near Plato del Mar reported a surprise. For a long time, escoria—strange, glassy formations—found in these cliffs had presented a puzzle. No one could explain the origin of the greenish glass or the red, brick-like material first discovered there in 1865. Now, a team of scientists pooled information gathered from other impact sites, especially Chicxulub.

The glass in the cliffs near Plato del Mar had formed almost 3.3 million years ago. At about the same time, several local species had suddenly become extinct. A giant armadillo that lived in the area suddenly disappeared from the fossil record. So did a flightless meat-eating bird and several kinds of ground sloths. In all, thirty-six species vanished.

Other studies show that a series of cooling cycles also began in the area 3.3 million years ago. When the researchers looked closely at the glass and brick-like material, they realized that it contained the signatures, or marks, of a powerful explosion. The glass also contains significant amounts of iridium. After putting all this evidence together, scientists came to the conclusion that a large impact had taken place in the area 3.3 million years ago.

Another discovery took place in January 1999. Researchers looking for oil 150 miles (240 km) off the northern coast of Norway reported a startling find. Using radar, they detected a large, extremely well-preserved impact crater under the Barents Sea. It is the "footprint" of a very large rock that hammered its way into the sea some 150 million years ago. It was named Mjølnir Crater, after the hammer hefted by Thor, the Norse god of thunder.

Further research showed that the 25-mile (40-km)-wide crater formed when an asteroid plunged into the sea. Rock samples drilled from nearby sites contained the telltale shocked quartz grains that signal a large impact. Researchers also found traces of iridium, the element so common in space and so uncommon here on Earth.

The asteroid may have been as large as 152 feet (50 m) across and traveled at a speed of 19,000 miles (30,500 km) per hour as it hurtled toward Earth. When the asteroid hit the water, a huge mushroom cloud of superheated steam must have spewed in all directions. Gigantic tidal waves most certainly inundated large areas of Canada and Russia. This major event, we can be sure, had a dramatic effect on life. The find is an important one. Of the 160 known impact craters on Earth, only seven have been found underwater, and this one is very well preserved.

Clearly, we have only begun to explore the evidence of past impacts and their consequences on the surface of our planet.

Chapter 3

What If It Happened Now?

What would happen if an asteroid the size of the Tunguska object hit St. Louis, Missouri, or Los Angeles, California, or Beijing, China? Nuclear bombs have taught us a lot about how huge explosions can damage life on Earth. We know that a blast "brighter than a thousand suns" can topple buildings, sear flesh, sever limbs, destroy lives and families, and scorch and burn vegetation.

Nuclear tests and computer simulations have shown us what even larger blasts could do. Grimly enough, the atomic bombs dropped on Hiroshima and Nagasaki in 1945 were far less powerful than the explosive energy released by the asteroid that exploded over Siberia in 1908.

In 1945, a nuclear bomb destroyed most of the buildings in Hiroshima and killed thousands of people.

If an Asteroid Hit Land

Because an asteroid has not hit Earth since humans evolved, it is difficult to know precisely how an asteroid impact would affect us. The best we can do is estimate the damage using computer models.

Scientists have run models of what would happen if, say, a 1,500-foot (460-m)-wide asteroid headed straight for Los Angeles, California. As the giant space rock blazed through the atmosphere, its brightness would blind people. As the killer rock approached, spontaneous fires would break out all over the city. Trees, shrubs, and homes would burst into flames. The blast of its explosion would destroy buildings and flatten houses.

The results of being hit by even such a medium-sized asteroid would be terrible beyond belief. People who lived through it would be traumatized for life. They would see other people seared by the fireball as it streaked through the atmosphere. Fiery debris thrown up into space by the impact would come tumbling back through the atmosphere in a nightmare of raining fire.

Darkness and cold caused by the cloud of smoke and debris would last for many months, resulting in an "impact winter." Earthquakes set off by the blast would send spasmodic shocks along fault lines. Acid rain would poison the land, and the protective ozone layer would be stripped from the atmosphere. Vaporized rock would release huge amounts of carbon dioxide, and global warming would follow the long impact winter.

According to French asteroid hunter Alain Maury, people who survive an asteroid impact would see the foundations of civilization crumble. Banking and food-distribution networks would disintegrate. In the midst of the panic, military and police forces would prove ineffective. "Trust—that all-important glue of civilization—would evaporate," Maury says, "and fear would rule."

If an Asteroid Hit Water

Suppose the *Earth-crossing asteroid* (crossing Earth's orbit) splashed down in the ocean instead of on land. Many people assume that if an asteroid hit the ocean, human civilization would be safe. In reality, if the object is big enough, an ocean hit could be even more devastating than a blast on land.

Imagine what would happen if an asteroid 3 miles (5 km) across hit the mid-Atlantic Ocean. Scientists using computers to model such a disaster predict that an ocean hit by an asteroid this size would produce a deadly tsunami. The tower of water would hurtle across the

An artist's representation of a tsunami, or giant sea wave, crashing on shore.

Atlantic toward the United States, hitting the continental shelf that extends outward from the shore. The shelf would slow the pace of the tsunami, but make it hundreds of feet taller.

A wall of water as high as the Empire State Building would tower over the coastline, only to crash mightily down on the coastal cities of Washington, D.C., New York, and Boston, as well as the communities of Long Island. The wall of churning water would crush cities, farms, and homes. Powerful waves would destroy the entire upper East Coast of the United States.

Floodwaters would cover the Appalachian Mountains and pour over the tidelands and inland valleys of Delaware, Maryland, and Virginia. On the other side of the Atlantic, the coasts of France and Portugal would be inundated too. Millions of people would die.

A New View of Our Place in the Universe

One of the most poignant legacies of the twentieth century may be humankind's new recognition of our vulnerability to cataclysmic cosmic impacts. Some researchers are now suggesting that past bombardments from space may have been responsible for the destruction of some ancient civilizations.

Between 2500 and 800 B.C., three Bronze Age civilizations seem to have disappeared without a trace. Until recently, no one had any ideas about what happened to them. Now some scientists think that cosmic impacts may be to blame. This theory may seem far-fetched at first, but researchers point out that people have a natural tendency to disregard high-consequence risks if they have a low probability.

How Bad Would It Be?

Vital Statistics

	Size of Object	Damage	Risk
LOCAL DISASTER	Up to twice the size of a football field	Local damage	1 per 100 years
NATIONAL DISASTER	600 feet to 1 mile (180 m to 1.6 km)	Large areas of land could be affected; civilization could be destroyed	1 per 10,000 to 1 million years
THE LONGEST WINTER	1 to 10 miles (1.6 to 16 km) across	A global impact winter would result; 25 percent of the population would be killed; government, trade, transportation, and utilities would be destroyed; food supply would be affected	1 per 1 million to 100 million years
DOOMSDAY HIT	More than 10 miles (16 km) across	Most of Earth's land surfaces and nearly all living things would be destroyed	1 per 100 million to 1 billion years

People often ignore risks. For example, they may choose to live in places that are susceptible to hurricanes and flooding.

For example, many people are willing to live in houses built on the slopes of volcanoes, along earthquake faults, in tornado lanes and hurricane paths, and on exposed peninsulas and low-lying islands. We know that natural disasters may occur, but because the chances of a disaster striking any one particular site are low, the decision to build in a potentially dangerous area doesn't seem too risky.

Major asteroid impacts are even less common than volcanoes and tornadoes, but they do happen. And when they do, they cause a lot of damage. In recent years, we have come to understand the real potential threat of asteroids.

Chapter 4

Where Do They Come From?

Asteroids have smashed into every planet and moon in our solar system, leaving behind impact scars and destruction. What exactly are these space rocks, and where do they come from? The story of asteroids began about 4.5 billion years ago, when the star we call the Sun was still very young. The planets of our solar system were born about that same time. The planets, their moons, and the asteroids all developed from the flattened, spinning disk of dust and debris that surrounded the Sun.

Every atom that now exists on Earth came from that dust cloud. Every atom of every object on Earth was once part of that disk, known as a solar nebula. Even your body is made up of atoms that came from the solar nebula. The iron in your blood was originally part of this

An artist's view of the solar nebula, or disk of dust and debris, from which the solar system formed

cloud and has existed since the beginning of time. The same is true of the sulfur in your skin and fingernails. Your teeth and bones contain primordial calcium. You are made of the same stuff as the planets, moons, and asteroids. Like everything else in the Universe, you are truly made of stardust.

But exactly how did that primitive dust cloud turn into a solar system full of planets, moons, rings, comets, and asteroids? Thanks to planetary spacecraft such as *Galileo, Voyager 1,* and *Voyager 2,* we now know that the solar system contains many other worlds. Each one is unique. How did all this variety come from one huge cloud of dust?

A popular theory proposes that the differences stemmed from relative distances from the Sun's heat and light. Different substances con-

Planets near the Sun, such as Mars (right), formed from heavier elements, such as metals; lighter gases often evaporated. Farther from the Sun, lighter gases did not evaporate, but instead formed the planets known as the gas giants, such as Saturn (below).

densed out of the nebula's grains of dust and vapor at different distances from the Sun. Near the Sun, only metals could condense out. Farther away, in the colder regions of the cloud, the lighter gases did not evaporate. Instead, they hung together and formed huge, gassy planets such as Jupiter and Saturn. These objects all orbited where they formed.

This simple view of the Universe's foundation was challenged in the 1980s when high-speed computers came along. Models created on this new generation of computers showed that the truth was much more complex. Once objects formed, they didn't always continue to orbit in place. Passing objects often pulled each other out of their original orbits. As objects wobbled and bobbled and smacked into one another, they often broke up. Then the broken pieces slammed into one another. The collisions sometimes scraped or knocked off outer layers, leaving inner cores exposed. The early solar system was a jumbled, unpredictable, and violent place.

By the time the adolescent planets had grown to about 1,000 miles (1,600 km) in diameter, things really started to get crazy. The objects in the solar system kept crashing into one another and then reassembling. Eventually, the relatively stable objects and orbits we see today formed.

When most of the commotion was over, Mars, Jupiter, and Saturn had captured many chunks of rock and metal. These satellites are what we call "moons." The rest of the debris in the solar system was either too small or too far away to form planets or become moons. Many of these objects became trapped in the *asteroid belt*—a broad region between Jupiter and Mars. This doughnut-shaped superhighway of orbiting rocks is about 184 million miles (300 million km) wide.

Thousands of asteroids orbit the Sun within this belt, and yet vast distances exist between them. Unlike scenes sometimes shown in movies, the asteroid belt is not packed tightly with spinning rocks. Spacecraft passing through the asteroid belt on their way to the outer solar system do not have to dodge swarms of obstacles. In fact, the asteroids in the asteroid belt are so far from one another that a person standing on the surface of one asteroid might occasionally see a distant light—looking a lot like a star—drifting across the nighttime sky. That light would be the Sun's reflection off the nearest asteroid neighbor.

The Ten Largest Asteroids
Vital Statistics

Asteroid	Diameter*	Average Distance from Sun (AU)+	Year of Discovery
1 CERES	584 miles (940 km)	2.77	1801
4 VESTA	358 miles (576 km)	2.36	1807
2 PALLAS	334 miles (538 km)	2.77	1802
10 HYGEIA	267 miles (430 km)	3.14	1849
704 INTERAMNIA	210 miles (338 km)	3.06	1910
511 DAVIDA	201 miles (323 km)	3.18	1903
65 CYBELE	191 miles (308 km)	3.43	1861
52 EUROPA	181 miles (292 km)	3.10	1858
87 SYLVIA	175 miles (282 km)	3.49	1866
451 PATIENTIA	175 miles (280 km)	3.06	1899

* 1 AU (*astronomical unit*) is the mean distance of Earth from the Sun, 93 million miles (150 million km)

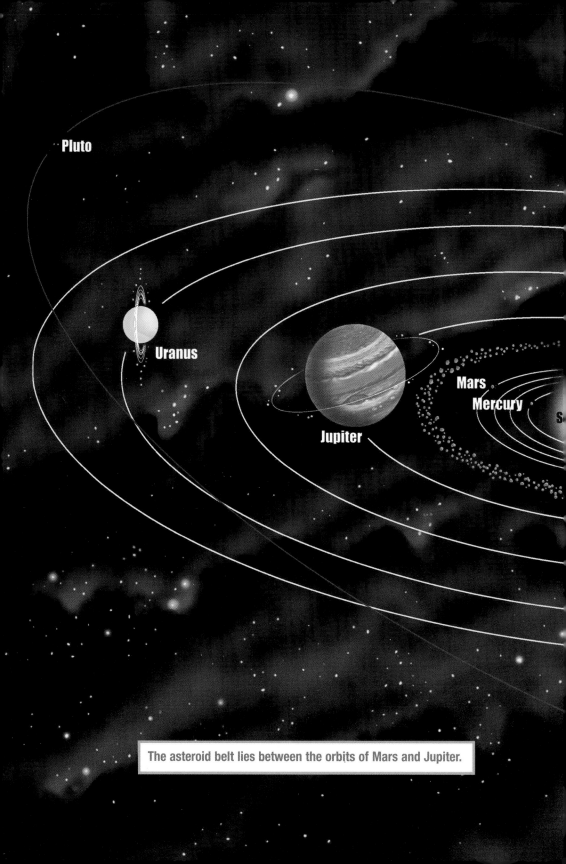

Pluto

Uranus

Mars
Mercury

Jupiter

S

The asteroid belt lies between the orbits of Mars and Jupiter.

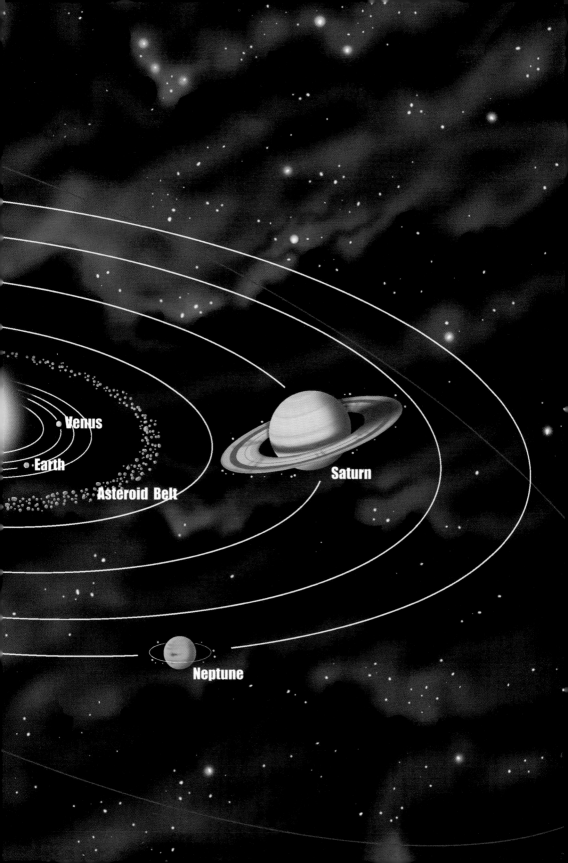

The word "asteroid" means "starlike," but an asteroid has very little in common with a star. A star is a huge ball of burning gases; an asteroid is a relatively small rock. A star generates its own heat and light; an asteroid can only bounce light off its dark, barren surface.

Because an asteroid is so different from a star, some scientists prefer to call these odd-shaped space rocks "minor planets." Like Earth, Mars, and Saturn, minor planets orbit the Sun and follow *elliptical* (oval-shaped) paths. Yet asteroids are much smaller than planets. The largest one—1 Ceres—is only 584 miles (940 km) across. That's about the distance from Portland, Oregon, to San Francisco, California. Most asteroids are much smaller than that, though, and some are the size of pebbles. Only sixteen known asteroids have a diameter of 149 miles (240 km) or more.

Outside the Belt

If you saw the films *Deep Impact* or *Armageddon*, you already know that not all asteroids are found in the asteroid belt. They are scattered all over the solar system, and a few of them come threateningly close to Earth.

Some, such as the big asteroid Chiron, cut a faraway path around the Sun. Chiron orbits beyond Jupiter in the outer solar system. Some scientists believe that the dark objects they have detected in a region called the Kuiper Belt, located beyond Pluto, are also asteroids. Another group of asteroids—called the Trojan Asteroids—orbit the Sun in the same orbit as Jupiter, some a little ahead and others a little behind the giant planet.

Yet another group of asteroids have orbits close to the orbits of Earth and Mars. They are known as near-Earth asteroids, or NEAs.*

* Because some comets orbit close to Earth, the term "near-Earth objects," or NEOs, is often used to refer to both asteroids and comets in this region.

In the movie *Armageddon*, a large chunk of an asteroid struck the Chrysler Building in New York City.

Although scientists have never observed an asteroid that is clearly headed straight for Earth, most experts think it's just a matter of time. Sooner or later, one of these close neighbors of ours will track a collision course for our planet.

Close Encounters of the Asteroid Kind

Based on where their orbits lie, nearby asteroids are divided into three main families: Amor asteroids, Apollo asteroids, and Aten asteroids. The vast majority have been discovered only recently, as technology has helped improve observation and as we have become more aware of the possibility of impact.

An artist's representation of the near-Earth asteroid 433 Eros

During the first 100 years of asteroid observation, astronomers discovered 463 asteroids, but only one orbited close to Earth. Spotted in 1898, it was named 433 Eros. It took 34 years to find another near-Earth asteroid.

Eros is another name for Cupid, so the second near-Earth asteroid was named 1221 Amor (the Latin word for "love"). Since then, scientists have spotted many more asteroids that, like 433 Eros and 1221 Amor, have orbits inside the orbit of Mars. Many of these asteroids cross that planet's orbit, but they don't cross Earth's path. This group of NEAs is now known as the Amor family of asteroids, named after the asteroid 1221 Amor. Eros is considered part of that family.

Scientists think that Mars may have drawn many Amor asteroids away—or *perturbed* them—from their original orbits within the main asteroid belt. Since the Amor asteroids now orbit close to Mars and Earth, the two planets continue to perturb these asteroids' orbits, and at present, no one is exactly sure how much. So, Amors could easily become Earth-crossing asteroids and could very well develop a collision path with Earth.

The Amor asteroids are not the only near-Earth asteroids. In 1932, the year 1221 Amor was identified, scientists spotted another kind of near-Earth asteroid—one that travels closer to the Sun than Earth does. They named it Apollo, after the Roman god of the Sun. The asteroid 1862 Apollo skims inside Earth's orbit, cuts across Earth's path, and then spends most of its time on the other side of our planet. In the next 17 years, astronomers discovered five more asteroids with orbits like Apollo's, and these asteroids became known as the Apollo family.

The size and location of Apollo asteroid orbits vary. Some Apollo asteroids also cross the orbits of Venus and Mars. The asteroid 1566 Icarus, a member of the Apollo family, veers far in toward the Sun. At some points in its orbit, it is less than half the distance of Mercury from the Sun's blast furnace. Skywatchers have found more than 250 Apollo asteroids so far.

In 1976, scientists noticed a new asteroid and named it Aten. They quickly realized that this asteroid has a different kind of orbit—one that remains mostly inside Earth's orbit. It travels around the Sun in less than 1 Earth-year. Only a few dozen Aten asteroids have been found so far. How many more exist? No one is quite sure. This family of NEAs is easy to miss because most of their paths run so close to the Sun that, from Earth, they are difficult to see in the brightness of day or the poor viewing conditions of twilight.

Could Aten asteroids that come very close to Earth's orbit pose a hazard? Some experts think so. Moreover, if these asteroids pass close to Venus in their journey, that planet's gravitational field could easily nudge them into an Earth-crossing pattern.

We now know that many dangerous objects lurk in our part of the solar system. Scientists want to know how many more Earth-crossing

Types of Near-Earth Asteroids

Vital Statistics

Asteroid Family	Named After	Orbit and Description	Examples
AMOR ASTEROIDS	1221 Amor, discovered in 1932	Asteroids that cross the orbit of Mars, but do not quite reach the orbit of Earth. Some may have been peturbed out of the main asteroid belt by Mars; others may be the nuclei of extinct comets. These asteroids may become Earth-crossing Apollo asteroids if they are perturbed by Mars or Earth.	433 Eros
APOLLO ASTEROIDS	1862 Apollo, discovered in 1932	Asteroids that cross Earth's orbit, but most of their path is beyond our planet's path. Some may be nuclei of extinct comets. They could impact Earth in the next million years.	1566 Icarus, 3200 Phaethon, 1620 Geographos
ATEN ASTEROIDS	2062 Aten, discovered in 1976	Asteroids that cross Earth's orbit, but most of their path is inside our planet's path. Their proximity to the Sun makes them difficult to spot during most of their orbital journey.	2062 Aten, 2100 Ra-Shalom

This painting helps people understand that many asteroids roam near Earth.

asteroids are out there and which ones may be a threat to our planet. How big are they? How much damage could they do? Most importantly, when will they hit? Teams of energetic and watchful researchers worldwide now scan the skies for potential signs of danger.

Chapter 5

Asteroids Close Up

For nearly 200 years, we had only tiny, fuzzy images of asteroids. Peering through telescopes from Earth, all we could see were small, indistinct objects. Scientists had to make all their observations through the veil of our planet's thick atmosphere, and many basic questions remained completely unanswered. What is the shape of asteroids? Are our ideas about their composition correct? How can we find out more about their orbits? With the 1990s, though, space-age investigations began to pay off with more information, and scientists began to get answers to these and many more questions about asteroids.

Gaspra and Ida

In 1991, the spacecraft *Galileo* visited an asteroid for the first time. Launched in 1989, *Galileo*'s primary mission was to explore Jupiter and its moons. As an added bonus, the National Aeronautics and Space Administration (NASA) succeeded in guiding Galileo close to two asteroids as the spacecraft passed through the asteroid belt.

First, *Galileo* passed by a small asteroid named 951 Gaspra. It is about half the size of Lake Tahoe on the California–Nevada border. Images taken by *Galileo* showed us that Gaspra is heavily pockmarked

This view of the asteroid Gaspra was created from images collected by Galileo.

with craters. Apparently, even asteroids get pounded by the flying debris of space. Much to our surprise, we also discovered that Gaspra's surface is covered with a thin layer of soil and fragments much like the layer of dust on the surface of our Moon. Dust of this kind is caused by erosion, produced by the constant, pounding bombardment of objects whizzing through space.

In 1993, *Galileo* flew by an irregularly-shaped asteroid known as 243 Ida. It is about three times longer than Gaspra. This time, a real surprise was in store for us: Orbiting around this little world was a tiny moon! No asteroid-moon combination had ever before been discov-

Galileo's images revealed the asteroid Ida's moon, Dactyl.

Newly discovered asteroids are given a temporary name that consists of the year of discovery and a distinguishing code, such as 1996JA1. Once the discovery is confirmed and the orbit is known, the asteroid receives an official name with two parts—a number and a more imaginative name.

The number comes first. Most people assume the number stands for the order of discovery, but actually the number indicates the order in which scientists have determined the orbits of known asteroids. The asteroid 1 Ceres, the first asteroid ever spotted, was discovered in 1801. Its orbit was also the first one confirmed, so its number is 1. People often omit the numeric part of the name, so you'll hear the name "Ceres" instead of 1 Ceres, or "Eros" instead of the more official 433 Eros.

The second part of most asteroid names follows one of several traditions. Some are named after minor gods and goddesses of classical times, such as Ceres (the Roman goddess of agriculture) or Icarus (a mythological character who flew too close to the Sun). A few recall other mythologies, such as 2062 Aten, named for an Egyptian god of the Sun. Others carry the name of a country, state, or city. Still others commemorate individuals, such as 3352 McAuliffe, named after Christa McAuliffe, the teacher who died in the *Challenger* Space Shuttle accident in January 1986. Some have frivolous names, and a few have even been named after pets.

ered, and this moon, named Dactyl, was so small scientists thought they might never have seen it from Earth. By October 1999, though, ground-based technology had improved enough to detect a moon orbiting an asteroid named 45 Eugenia. It is likely that scientists will discover more asteroid-orbiting moons in the future.

Visit to a Near-Earth Asteroid

In 1996, NASA launched the *Near-Earth Asteroid Rendezvous (NEAR)* mission to explore two asteroids. It later became known as *NEAR Shoemaker*, in memory of asteroid hunter Eugene Shoemaker (1928–1997). In 1997, *NEAR* flew by the asteroid 253 Mathilde and then continued on for the major goal of its mission—to spend a year orbiting the asteroid 433 Eros, a large near-Earth asteroid in the Amor family.

Mathilde is a carbon-rich asteroid in the main asteroid belt. *NEAR* passed within 750 miles (1,200 km) of this medium-sized asteroid. The spacecraft's images revealed large, cavernous craters gouged deeply into the asteroid's charcoal-colored surface.

After leaving the dark world of Mathilde, *NEAR* continued toward 433 Eros for our first close-up view of a near-Earth asteroid. *NEAR* began its 1-year study in February 2000. NASA originally intended for *NEAR* to begin orbiting 433 Eros in 1999, but scientists had to postpone the rendezvous when they unexpectedly lost contact with *NEAR* at a critical moment in late 1998. NASA quickly regained contact with the spacecraft and reprogrammed it for a more distant flyby. Then they rerouted the spacecraft to swing back later for its year-long study.

NEAR provided the information that scientists used to create this view of the asteroid Mathilde.

We've all seen spectacular photographs of faraway moons and planets taken by *Viking* or *Voyager* or *Galileo,* but imaging cameras aren't the only way—or even the most important way—that a spacecraft tells us about an object in space. Besides a camera, *NEAR* carried six scientific instruments into space. These instruments can provide reams of important data.

How strong is the *magnetic field* of the asteroid? What is its orientation? Does its magnetic field come from a magnetic core within, or is it left over from some part of the asteroid's history? The answers to these questions will come from an instrument called a magnetometer, which will measure the asteroid's magnetic field.

Other instruments onboard *NEAR* will allow the mission's science team to figure out the asteroid's *mass*—the amount of material it contains—as well as its shape, what its surface looks like, what kinds of minerals it contains, and how long it was exposed to extreme bombardment. If sci-entists observe evidence of geological processes, such as volcano eruptions and earthquakes, they will know that the chunk of rock was originally part of a much larger object.

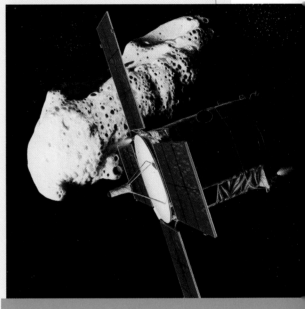

An artist's representation of *NEAR* visiting Eros

Asteroid Family Tree

In July 1999, a small spacecraft known as *Deep Space 1* flew close to a near-Earth asteroid named 9969 Braille. It was the closest flyby ever made. The spacecraft came within 16 miles (26 km) of Braille.

Right after its closest approach, *Deep Space 1* trained its infrared camera on Braille and made a startling discovery. Braille may be a chip

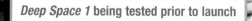

Deep Space 1 being tested prior to launch

off an old block. It may once have been a part of 4 Vesta, one of the largest objects in the asteroid belt. Both asteroids have high concentrations of a mineral found in very few asteroids. Braille is small—only about 1.3 miles (2.1 km) on its longest side and 0.6 miles (1 km) on its short side—and it will probably travel back near Earth in a few thousand years.

Roving and Sampling the Surface

Because building spacecraft and planning missions takes so much time, NASA and other space agencies have already started work on spacecraft that will reach their destinations many years from now. In 2006, the MUSES-C mission, a joint effort between Japan and the United States, will pay a visit to the near-Earth asteroid 4660 Nereus.

The spacecraft will contain a robot land rover supplied by NASA. Like the rover that explored Mars during the Pathfinder mission of 1997, the MUSES-C rover will land on the asteroid and crawl across its surface. As the rover rumbles about, it will examine the asteroid's features, rocks, and dust. Nereus has far less *gravity* than either the Moon or Mars, though, so landing will present an interesting challenge.

MUSES-C will also send samples from the surface of Nereus back to Earth. Scientists will then use high-tech laboratory techniques to analyze the asteroid samples. For a long time, scientists have strongly suspected that there is a relationship between asteroids and the meteorites that tumble to Earth's surface. By examining samples collected on Nereus, scientists may finally be able to determine whether meteorites are made of material that has chipped off asteroids.

The European Space Agency has planned and sponsored the *ROSETTA* project. Although designed primarily to visit and study

How are asteroids different from comets? People talk about finding meteorites on Earth. How are meteorites different from meteors, and what's the difference between a meteoroid and an asteroid?

Three related words cause a lot of confusion: *meteoroid*, *meteor*, and meteorite. A meteoroid is a small object made of rock and metal that travels through space. Scientists believe that meteoroids are pieces of material that have been knocked off asteroids or comets—or sometimes planets such as Mars. A meteor is the streak of light that appears briefly in the sky when a meteoroid speeds into Earth's atmosphere. Most meteoroids burn up completely before they reach Earth's surface. However, when these objects strike Earth's surface, they are called meteorites.

Scientists used to think that the distinction between asteroids and comets was very clear, but lately it has become a little blurry. For one thing, some asteroids appear to be burned-out comets. However, most comets have a loosely packed nucleus of dirt, rock, and water ice. They also have very large, elliptical orbits that often extend far out beyond the orbit of Pluto on one end and inward toward the Sun on the other end. When a comet comes close to the Sun, it develops a *coma* or "tail" of vaporized water that glistens with reflected sunlight.

The chunk of rock that causes a meteor (left) will become a meteorite (above) if it lands on Earth's surface.

Missions to Explore Asteroids
Vital Statistics

Mission	Year of Launch	Year of Encounter	Asteroid Visited	Country of Origin
GALILEO	1989	1991	951 Gaspra	United States
		1993	243 Ida	
NEAR EARTH ASTEROID RENDEZVOUS (NEAR)	1996	1997	253 Mathilde	United States
		2000	433 Eros	United States
DEEP SPACE 1 (DS1)	1998	1999	9969 Braille	United States
MUSES-C	2002 (planned)	2003 (planned)	4660 Nereus	Japan and United States
ROSETTA	2003 (planned)	2006 (planned)	4979 Otawara	European Space Agency (ESA)

Comet Wirtanen, the spacecraft will also visit two asteroids in the main asteroid belt. In 2006, it will fly by the asteroid 4979 Otawara. In 2008, *ROSETTA* will pass by 140 Siwa. Siwa is believed to be a very old, carbon-rich asteroid. Scientists currently know very little about these two asteroids, but after *ROSETTA*'s visit, they should know a great deal more.

While visits to asteroids will help us better understand the Universe we live in, they also serve an immediate practical purpose: They give us information about the structure of asteroids—just in case we ever need to divert or destroy an asteroid that is on a crash course for Earth. The other ongoing challenge we face is finding all the asteroids that could be headed our way.

Chapter 6

Looking Out for Danger

The first rule of self-defense is to know your opponent. While our robot spacecraft gather information about known asteroids, teams of scientists on Earth are scanning the skies to locate more—especially ones that might pose a threat to our planet. These researchers face a formidable challenge. Asteroids are small, faint objects. That makes them hard to find and difficult to track. It takes a winning combination of the best astronomers and high-tech equipment to do the job well.

Who's Watching?

So far, scientists have spotted only about 250 of the 500 to 1,000 or more near-Earth asteroids that probably exist. That means we know

Scientists working at the NEAT observation site at the U.S. Air Force's Space Surveillance Site atop Mt. Haleakala, Maui are searching the skies for asteroids.

nothing at all about 50 to 75 percent of the objects experts believe are orbiting near our planet. We have no idea what their orbits are, or whether any of them is on a crash course with Earth.

Now for the really bad news—locating a near-Earth object (NEO) is only the first step in a very long process. Once researchers have found a large NEO, they need to track its orbit for at least 20 years before they can be sure it will not collide with our planet.

Awareness of the potential danger is increasing. Searches now operate in many countries, and teams in the United States hope to coordinate more and more closely with their counterparts worldwide. The United States Congress has recently begun to recognize the need for more information about asteroids that could, without our knowledge, now be aimed directly at Earth. The United States Air Force has become involved in the effort and has offered new resources to skywatchers.

The scientific communities and governments of other countries have also begun cooperative efforts. Best of all, scientists have begun to find ways to conduct searches with greater speed and accuracy. Nevertheless, these triumphs represent only small successes when you consider the overall magnitude and importance of the project.

The Astronomer's Bag of Tricks

By the late 1990s, astronomers observing from the ground no longer depended on bigger and better optical telescopes alone. Their tools had grown to include photography, computer chip technology, and radar imaging, to name only a few.

At the dawn of the nineteenth century, when Giuseppe Piazzi discovered the first asteroid—1 Ceres—astronomers looked directly through the telescope eyepiece and sketched what they saw. By the mid-1800s, though, photography had made the astronomer's job much simpler, especially for finding small, faint objects like asteroids. A photographic plate could be made instantly and accurately. Plates were more sensitive to light than the human eye and could pick up types of light that the human eye could not. Astronomers used long exposure times to gather even more light.

In 1780, the government of Naples (now in Italy, but then an independent state) built two astronomical observatories—one in the city of Naples and one in Palermo. Giuseppe Piazzi, a Theatine monk, was put in charge of both observatories.

Piazzi had been trained in philosophy, but was intrigued by mathematics and astronomy. He traveled to France and England to learn how to run an observatory. During his trip, he visited the great amateur astronomer William Herschel in England. As he was climbing up the ladder to Herschel's huge telescope, Piazzi fell and broke his arm, but that did not deter him.

When the observatory at Palermo was completed, Piazzi set to work. By 1814, he had mapped the locations of 7,646 stars and had made several interesting discoveries. However, his most exciting contribution had nothing to do with stars.

In 1781, Herschel had discovered the planet Uranus. Suddenly, astronomers all over the world started to look for more planets. Herschel had found Uranus in exactly the position predicted by a mathematical calculation called Bode's law. That same rule predicted that another planet orbited somewhere between the orbits of Mars and Jupiter, and that's what everyone, including Piazzi, began to search for.

Piazzi is the one who found—well, not a planet, exactly. It was much too puny to be called a planet, so it was called an asteroid and received the name 1 Ceres.

Giuseppe Piazzi

Next, scientists began connecting motors to their telescopes so the telescopes moved at the same speed that Earth rotates. This way, the background stars appeared as single dots on the plate, while an orbiting asteroid showed up as a streak of light. By making consistent exposures and comparing photographic plates from different sessions, astronomers could look for streaks and find asteroids much more easily. The result was a big increase in asteroid discoveries. Between 1845 and 1903, 500 asteroids were discovered.

Today, high-sensitivity charged coupling devices (CCDs) are replacing photographic plates, and computers have taken over for the human eyes that once scanned the plates for streaks of light. Information now goes straight from the light-sensitive CCD to the computer. The computer screens out "noise"—similar to radio static or snow on a TV screen. It also recognizes known asteroids and weeds them out of

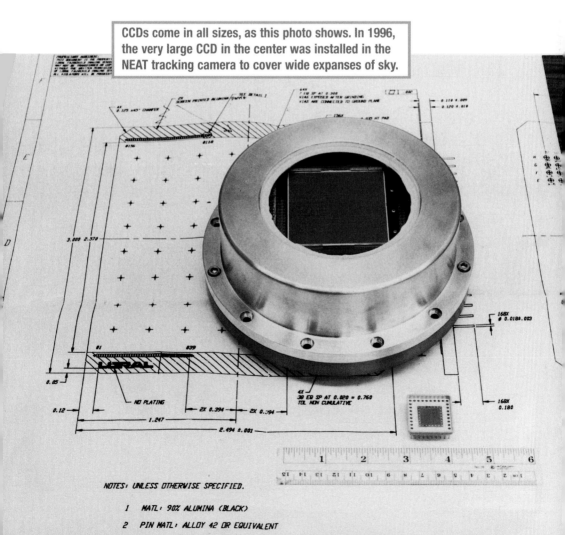

CCDs come in all sizes, as this photo shows. In 1996, the very large CCD in the center was installed in the NEAT tracking camera to cover wide expanses of sky.

NOTES: UNLESS OTHERWISE SPECIFIED.

1   MATL: 90% ALUMINA (BLACK)

2   PIN MATL: ALLOY 42 OR EQUIVALENT

the results. In addition, the computer can recognize "space garbage"—orbiting debris produced by both human activity and the cosmos. In this way, real asteroids can be located quickly and accurately. This high-tech system has caused a revolution in asteroid discovery. By 1998, the total number of known asteroids had climbed well beyond 8,500.

One relatively new astronomy tool is particularly useful for observing asteroids, especially when they pass close to Earth. Using large *radio telescopes*, astronomers can bounce *radar* waves off the passing asteroids to determine their shape. The waves that return allow scientists to make three-dimensional maps of the asteroids. From these returning echoes, they can also predict what the asteroid is made of, measure its rotation, and determine some information about its orbit.

In other words, radio telescopes provide exactly the kind of information scientists would need to deflect an asteroid headed for our planet. Most radio telescopes use a huge metal "dish" to collect radio waves and focus them on a large rod, or antenna, in the center. Operators can direct the antenna toward any point in the sky. By August 1998, more than 40 NEAs had been detected using radio telescopes.

Asteroid Hunting Teams

Traditionally, asteroid searches—for NEOs and farther-off asteroids—have been done primarily by amateurs, volunteers, and scientists given only tiny slivers of time on large observatory telescopes.

The real pioneers in searching for near-Earth asteroids in the United States were Eugene Shoemaker and Eleanor Helin. When they began a program at the Hale Observatories on Mt. Palomar, California, in the 1970s, they had only 1 week each month to scan the skies using one of the observatory's small telescopes. Yet the team they put together made

A Sampling of Earth-Based Surveys

Vital Statistics

Project Name	Location	Directed By	Equipment Used	Date Begun
LINEAR (LINCOLN NEAR-EARTH ASTEROID RESEARCH PROGRAM)	Socorro, New Mexico	Massachusetts Institute of Technology (MIT) and the U.S. Air Force	36-inch (91-cm) tracking telescope at the White Sands Missile Range, New Mexico	1997
LONEOS (LOWELL OBSERVATORY NEAR-EARTH OBJECT SURVEY)	Flagstaff, Arizona	NASA and Lowell Observatory	23-inch (58-cm) Schmidt telescope and CCD camera	1998
NEAT (NEAR-EARTH ASTEROID TRACKING)	Pasadena, California	NASA's Jet Propulsion Laboratory (JPL) and the U.S. Air Force	36-inch (91-cm) Air Force telescope on the island of Maui, Hawaii	1996
SPACEWATCH	Tucson, Arizona	Kitt Peak National Observatory, University of Arizona	36-inch (91-cm) Newtonian reflector telescope, CCD camera, and automated search	1981

Eleanor "Glo" Helin

Eleanor F. Helin—known as "Glo"—could be called the Queen of Near-Earth Asteroids. Helin has been active in planetary science and astronomy for more than three decades. For most of that time, she has been working for NASA's Jet Propulsion Laboratory (JPL) in Pasadena, California, and the California Institute of Technology (Caltech). She is currently in charge of NASA/JPL's Near Earth Asteroid Tracking (NEAT) program, which has had great success at finding near-Earth asteroids.

In the early 1970s, Helin pioneered a program to track planet-crossing asteroids at Caltech's Palomar Observatory. That program found thousands of space objects of all types—including 100 near-Earth asteroids and 20 comets. In fact, Helin personally discovered the first Aten asteroid—2926 Aten—in 1976. Aten asteroids are especially hard to find because they orbit the Sun inside Earth's orbit, so skywatchers must look toward the Sun's bright light as they search. Another of Helin's asteroid discoveries, 9969 Braille, was the flyby target for NASA/JPL's *Deep Space 1* spacecraft.

Helin is recognized around the world for her work in asteroid science. In fact, the International Astronomical Union named the asteroid 3267 Helin in her honor. NASA honored her with an Exceptional Service Medal and the 1997 JPL Award for Excellence for her leadership of the NEAT program. In 1998, she was inducted into the Women in Science and Technology International (WITI) Hall of Fame.

many of the first 200 near-Earth asteroid discoveries.* More recent high-tech programs have built on the shoulders of these pioneers.

Today, teams of astronomers all over the world are using electronic cameras and telescopes to survey the sky for NEOs. The group of researchers is still small, though. In 1999, fewer than 100 people were involved! The most productive current searches include Spacewatch at Kitt Peak Observatory in Arizona and a group of projects with alphabet-soup names like LINEAR, NEAT, and LONEOS.

* The team later included Gene's wife, Carolyn Shoemaker, who co-discovered Comet Shoemaker-Levy 9.

Chapter 7

What Should We Do?

Since 1980, when scientists realized that a cosmic impact killed the dinosaurs, we've come to recognize that killer asteroids and comets are a reality of the past. Some overreactions were sure to occur. In March 1998, calculations made by a watchful astronomer led him to announce that we had 20 years to prepare for a collision with a little-known asteroid named 1997 XF11. Newspaper headlines blared. TV news announcers led with the story. Scientists and engineers began to calculate whether we had enough time to prevent or lessen the disaster.

The next day, however, new calculations came from another group of astronomers. When they heard the announcement, these scientists searched their archives, found previous images of the asteroid 1997 XF11, and used them to predict the asteroid's orbit more accurately. The second team announced that the asteroid would come close, but not nearly close enough to be a threat. Everyone breathed a sigh of relief.

To avoid confusion and unnecessary panic, space scientists have devised the Torino scale for comparing impact events. The scale measures the likelihood of an asteroid or comet impact and its potential damage. Like the Richter scale for earthquakes, the Torino scale provides a common frame of reference for talking about the seriousness of a possible collision with Earth. The scale was endorsed by the International Astronomical Union in 1999.

The Torino Scale

Events having no likely consequences	0	The likelihood of a collision is zero or well below the chance that a random object of the same size will strike Earth within the next few decades. This designation also applies to any small object that, in the event of a collision, is unlikely to reach Earth's surface intact.
Events meriting careful monitoring	1	The chance of collision is extremely unlikely, about the same as a random object of the same size striking Earth within the next few decades.
Events meriting concern	2	A somewhat close, but not unusual encounter. Collision is very unlikely.
	3	A close encounter, with 1 percent or greater chance of a collision capable of causing localized destruction.
	4	A close encounter, with 1 percent or greater chance of a collision capable of causing regional devastation.
Threatening events	5	A close encounter, with a significant threat of a collision capable of causing regional devastation.
	6	A close encounter, with a significant threat of a collision capable of causing global catastrophe.
	7	A close encounter, with an extremely significant threat of a collision capable of causing global catastrophe.
Certain collisions	8	A collision capable of causing localized destruction. Such events occur somewhere on Earth once every 50 to 1,000 years.
	9	A collision capable of causing regional devastation. Such events occur between once every 1,000 to 100,000 years.
	10	A collision capable of causing a global climatic catastrophe. Such events occur once every 100,000 years or less.

In April 1999, another alarm sounded. Skywatchers on the LIN-EAR team spotted a new asteroid, 1999 AN10. A team of scientists in Italy made calculations based on multiple sightings, but couldn't verify their findings because the 1-mile (1.6-km)-wide asteroid moved into a portion of its orbit where it couldn't be seen from Earth. The Italian scientists speculated that 1999 AN10 might come close enough to Earth in 2029 to be perturbed, possibly causing a collision in 2039. If this scenario were correct, we would have only 40 years to prepare.

Obviously, the time has come to take asteroids seriously. Critical discussions of the cosmic impact problem have involved the United Nations, government representatives from around the world, and experts in various scientific disciplines. Most participants believe that we need to accomplish three major goals.

1. We must improve our ability to identify potential Earth-crossers. Our first and best defense against these disasters is to locate all the near-Earth asteroids that measure 0.6 mile (1 km) or larger and identify the paths they follow. To do this, we need more researchers, equipment, and funding, and we need worldwide cooperation.

2. We must learn as much as we can about the nature of asteroids through every means available, including robot exploration.

3. We must identify and develop ways to divert or destroy objects headed for Earth in time to save our planet and ourselves.

Calling All Watchers

The first of these goals is most important. If we do not identify potentially hazardous asteroids, there's no point in developing ways to divert or destroy them. The number of people worldwide who are currently

The arrow on the lower right of this photograph shows a new object detected by an asteroid tracking system.

watching for collision-course asteroids and comets would barely be enough to staff a fast-food restaurant. Watches in progress often have to be shut down for lack of funding and for lack of time available on existing equipment.

We need to develop a serious, worldwide network that covers the entire sky with an organized, well-planned scan. With the recent improvements in technology, this network should greatly increase our knowledge of the near-Earth objects that cross our planet's path. If scientists find an asteroid or comet that's headed straight for us, they'll need a lot of time to collect information about it. They'll have to calculate the asteroid's size and speed, its precise orbit, what part of Earth it is most likely to hit, and its angle of approach.

Many asteroid search teams are focused now on locating the largest objects because they could do the most harm. However, as we have seen, smaller objects can also cause great devastation.

Recent observational improvements have increased astronomers' abilities to predict asteroid orbits accurately. Computerized computation and modeling have also made this tricky process much more precise. A firm prediction requires multiple observations, however, and that's not always easy. Once an asteroid has been spotted, it may disappear from view for many reasons.

Many near-Earth asteroids are extremely faint objects—both very small and dark. Because their orbits vary so greatly, just obtaining a second sighting can present a big challenge. Because Aten asteroids travel close to the Sun, they are obscured by sunlight during some parts of their orbit. These asteroids are potentially extremely dangerous because they may go unobserved until they are nearly on our doorstep. The case of 1997 XF11 shows just how tricky getting accurate calculations can be.

Once Warned, Then What?

What should we do if scientists suddenly spot an asteroid headed straight for Earth? In other words, what is our plan of defense?

Many people think it would be best to evacuate the impact area, but this would only be possible if the incoming object were very small. Even if evacuation was a viable option, just imagine the chaos involved

Frightened residents flee the coast in the movie *Deep Impact*.

in moving everyone out of an entire city or state. Highways and freeways would be jammed. Panic would set in. People would be injured, possibly even killed in the rush for safety.

Once evacuees had arrived in a safe area, shortages of food and shelter would set in, as they do in any refugee camp. Water supplies could be tainted. Freezing-cold temperatures caused by clouds of *ejecta* and ash would block out the Sun and cause further hardship and death. The ecosystem of the hit area would be destroyed—plant and animal life would be obliterated. The ground would be scorched by fire, and the evacuees would have no homes or jobs or schools to return to. The economic and social damage would be greater than anything we've ever seen. That is why it is so important for us to be able to intercept an incoming asteroid before it hits Earth.

If the asteroid is small enough, we might be able to blow it up with nuclear explosives. Of course, this would have to be done with enormous care. Otherwise, a rain of shattered radioactive debris might end up causing hundreds of deadly impacts scattered over a wide area. Also, this strategy would require launching nuclear explosives from Earth, which in itself could be hazardous. Ironically, this positive use for nuclear devices comes at a time when we have been working to save the world from nuclear disaster by discouraging nuclear arms development.

For a larger object, it would be better to set off an explosion nearby. Careful detonation could nudge the asteroid into a new, nonthreatening orbit. One expert suggests exploding a nuclear bomb directly in front of the incoming intruder to alter its orbit. Knowing exactly the right amount and placement of the charge would depend on having exact information about the asteroid's size and shape and the path it was following. This is where differences in composition could make a big difference. During an explosion, an object consisting of a pile of rubble would react much differently from a solid ball of nickel-iron.

David Williams, an asteroid expert at University College in London, England, has a different idea. He suggests landing a spacecraft with a solar-powered engine on the asteroid. The solar cells would trap sunlight and use the energy to power an ion gun that would give the asteroid a light, steady push—just enough to nudge the object out of its current orbit and prevent a collision with Earth.

Some experts claim that none of these plans would have any hope of success, unless we develop more effective propulsion systems.

An artist's view of using nuclear missiles to nudge an asteroid off-course

Imagine how you would feel if you knew that an asteroid was on a crash course with Earth. Even if the governments of the world could offer you hope that a plan to save the world was in place, no one would be able to guarantee that the plan would work. It would seem like the "end of the world" was coming. Doomsday would have a date, and whether that date was a month, a year, or 20 years away, the specter of the approaching asteroid would cast a shadow over everyone in the world.

Of course, not all people would react to the news in the same way. Some would pray, and others would panic. Some would be determined to live what might be their final days with as much dignity and peace as they could find. Others would choose to spend their last days satisfying their every desire. Churches would fill up, but so would the streets, the bars, and the low-life haunts.

Unfortunately, the worst possible scenario may be the most likely. In many places, as the asteroid drew closer, law would break down and the thin fabric of civilization would be torn to shreds. Rape, looting, and riots would ravage cities and towns. Burning and devastation would destroy property. Violence would take its toll on people. People in the military and law enforcement would simply throw up their hands, making their own choices on how to spend these days in limbo.

Of course, many people would not become barbaric in those final days. Instead they would turn to the solace of families and loved ones. But they would suffer too. Food and supplies would be hoarded and difficult to find. Essential services, such as electricity and running water, might simply cease to exist. Work would stop and the economy would crumble.

This is a worst-case scenario, but it's not unlikely. That is why some people in authority have suggested that it might be wiser not to inform the public as our fate hurtles toward us. Others point out that mass media and the Internet make secrecy practically impossible. Still others say that the public has a right to know of the possible danger and that we must trust humanity to conduct itself in accordance with our established laws and traditions of moral and civil behavior.

The truth is, we currently have no plan in place for preventing an asteroid from smashing into our planet. Hopefully, given time, we will be able to develop the right plan and use our technology to save our world. The question is, will we have the time? Will humankind go the way of the dinosaur, or will we be able to save ourselves? Only time will tell.

Exploring Asteroids: A Timeline

1801 — The first asteroid, 1 Ceres, is discovered.

1802 — The second asteroid, 2 Pallas, is discovered.

1898 — 433 Eros, the first near-Earth asteroid, is discovered.

1908 — Midair explosion of a stony asteroid near Tunguska, Siberia

1932 — Discovery of the second near-Earth asteroid, 1221 Amor, and the first Earth-crossing asteroid, 1862 Apollo

1976 — Discovery of 2062 Aten, the first of a family of asteroids with orbits mostly inside Earth's orbit

1980 — Luis Alvarez and his team announce their theory that an asteroid or comet impact caused the extinction of the dinosaurs 65 million years ago.

1981 — Spacewatch, a NASA-supported asteroid watch operated by the University of Arizona at Kitt Peak National Observatory near Tucson, Arizona, is founded.

1991 — *Galileo* spacecraft visits 951 Gaspra; the 1947 discovery of Chicxulub Crater on the Yucatan Peninsula is finally announced to the scientific community.

1993 — *Galileo* spacecraft visits 243 Ida and makes the first discovery of a moon orbiting an asteroid. The moon is named Dactyl.

1995 — A researcher at UCLA finds a small meteorite in Pacific Ocean sediment that may be part of the object that killed the dinosaurs 65 million years ago.

1996 — *Near Earth Asteroid Rendezvous (NEAR) Shoemaker* mission is launched; NEAT, a NASA-run asteroid watch team with observatory time on Air Force telescope on Maui, Hawaii, is founded.

1997 — *NEAR Shoemaker* spacecraft encounters 253 Mathilde. LINEAR, an NEO survey run by Lincoln Laboratory of MIT and the U.S. Air Force, is founded.

1998 — *Deep Space 1* (DS1) is launched to visit the asteroid 9969 Braille. LONEOS is established by NASA and

Lowell Observatory near Flagstaff, Arizona, to make a NEO survey.

2000 — *NEAR Shoemaker* begins a 1-year study as it orbits 433 Eros.

2002 — *MUSES-C* scheduled to head for the asteroid 4660 Nereus.

2003 — Europe's *ROSETTA* spacecraft scheduled to begin its journey to Comet Wirtanen. On the way, it will visit two asteroids—4979 Otawara (in 2006) and 140 Siwa (in 2008).

asteroid—a piece of rocky debris left over from the formation of the solar system 4.6 billion years ago. Most asteroids orbit the Sun in a belt between Mars and Jupiter.

asteroid belt—the region in space between Mars and Jupiter where most asteroids are found. It is 184 million miles (300 million km) wide.

astronomical unit (AU)—the mean distance of Earth from the Sun—1 AU = 93 million miles (150 million km). This measurement is often used to express distances within the solar system.

coma—the head of a comet, consisting of a nucleus of frozen water and rock

comet—a small ball of rock and ice that travels toward the Sun in a long orbit that originates on the remote outer edge of the solar system

core—the innermost region of a moon, planet, asteroid, or other object in space

crater—an irregular circular or oval depression in the surface of a planet, moon, asteroid, or ther object in space. It is made by a collision with another object.

crust—the outer surface of a moon, planet, asteroid, or other object in space

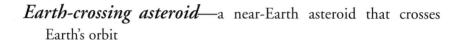

Earth-crossing asteroid—a near-Earth asteroid that crosses Earth's orbit

ejecta—one or more pieces of material thrown out, or ejected, from a crater site by the impact of an object

elliptical—oval; having the kind of shape achieved when you loop a string around two tacks, use a pencil to stretch the string to the third point in a triangle, and then, with the string always stretched taut, draw a perimeter around the focal points formed by the tacks

gravity—the force that pulls objects toward the center of a planet

magnetic field—the area in which a natural attractive force exists between a magnetic object and specific other substances, such as iron. The Earth possesses a magnetic field.

mantle—a geologically unique region below the crust and above the core of a moon or planet

mass—the amount of material in an object

meteor—the glowing light we see in the night sky when a meteoroid is in contact with Earth's atmosphere

meteorite—a chunk of dust or rock from space that strikes the surface of another object, such as a moon or planet

meteoroid—a rocky or metallic object of relatively small size, usually once part of a comet or asteroid

perturb—to disturb or upset

radar—radio detecting and ranging; a device that emits radio waves and anlayzes their reflections. Radar is often used to learn more about an object's surface features.

radio telescope—a telescope designed to gather radio waves. It usually has a large dish that focuses gathered waves on an antenna at the center.

retrograde—in the opposite direction from usual, that is, as seen from Earth, having an apparent westward movement; may be the result of an enormous, cataclysmic impact at some point in the past

satellite—any object that orbits another object in space. The Moon is a satellite of Earth, and Earth is a satellite of the Sun. Human-made satellites are called "artificial" to distinguish them from natural satellites, such as moons.

sediment—matter deposited by water, wind, or glaciers

tsunami—a giant tidal wave

To Find Out More

The news from space changes fast, so it's always a good idea to check the copyright date on books, CD-ROMs, and video tapes to make sure that you are getting up-to-date information. One good place to look for current information from NASA is U.S. government depository libraries. There are several in each state.

Books

Barnes-Svarney, Patricia. *Asteroid: Earth Destroyer or New Frontier?* New York: Plenum Press, 1996.

Campbell, Ann Jeanette. *The New York Public Library Amazing Space: A Book of Answers for Kids.* New York: John Wiley & Sons, 1997.

Dickinson, Terence. *Other Worlds: A Beginner's Guide to Planets and Moons.* Willowdale, Ontario: Firefly Books, 1995.

Gribbin, John and Mary. *Fire on Earth: Doomsday, Dinosaurs, and Humankind.* New York: St. Martin's Press, 1996.

Gustafson, John. *Planets, Moons and Meteors.* (The Young Stargazer's Guide to the Galaxy) New York: Julian Messner, 1992.

Hartmann, William K. and Don Miller. *The Grand Tour.* New York: Workman Publishing, 1993.

Lewis, John S. *Mining the Sky.* Reading, MA: Addison-Wesley, 1996.

_____. *Rain of Iron and Ice: The Very Real Threat of Comet and Asteroid Bombardment.* Reading, MA: Helix Books, 1996-1997.

Mechler, Gary (Editor), Steven Kent, Dr. Croft, Melinda Hutson. *Planets and Their Moons.* (National Audubon Society Pocket Guides) New York: Alfred Knopf, 1995.

Norton, O. Richard. *Rocks from Space, Second Edition.* Missoula: Mountain Press Publishing Company, 1998.

Powell, James Lawrence. *Night Comes to the Cretaceous: Dinosaur Extinction and the Transformation of Modern Geology.* New York: W. H. Freeman and Co., 1998.

Spangenburg, Ray, and Diane Moser. *Exploring the Reaches of the Solar System.* (Space Exploration) New York: Facts On File, Inc., 1990.

Verschuur, Gerrit L. *Impact! The Threat of Comets & Asteroids.* New York: Oxford University Press. 1996.

Vogt, Gregory L. *The Solar System Facts and Exploration.* Scientific American Sourcebooks. New York: Twenty-First Century Books, 1995.

CD-ROMs

Beyond Planet Earth. Discovery Channel School Multimedia, P.O. Box 970, Oxon Hill, MD, 20750-0970.
An interactive journey to Mars and beyond. Includes video from NASA and Voyager missions and more than 200 photographs.

Impact: Ground Zero. Bamboole, Inc., 1702-H Meridian Avenue, #102; San Jose, CA 95125; *http://www.cdanddvd.com/index.html.* Explores the science behind comet and asteroid impacts on Earth, with hundreds of photographs and illustrations from NASA archives. Includes interviews with key NASA asteroid experts and more than 200 pages of text.

Video Tape

Discover Magazine: Solar System, Discovery Channel School, P.O. Box 970, Oxon Hill, MD 20750-0970.

Organizations and Online Sites

Many of the sites listed on the following pages are NASA sites, with links to many other interesting sources of information about moons and planetary systems. You can also sign up to receive NASA news on many subjects via e-mail.

Astronomical Society of the Pacific
390 Ashton Avenue
San Francisco, CA 94112
http://www.aspsky.org

The Astronomy Café
http://www2.ari.net/home/odenwald/cafe.html
This site answers questions and offers news and articles related to astronomy and space. It is maintained by NASA scientist Sten Odenwald.

Expanding Universe—A Classified Search
Tool for Amateur Astronomy
http://www.mtrl.toronto.on.ca/centres/bsd/astronomy/523_44.HTM
This one-stop shopping site includes links to nearly two dozen excellent sites carrying information about asteroids from introductory to technical.

Information for Amateur Astronomers
http://asteroid.lowell.edu/asteroid/loneos/amateurs.html
Provides information for those amateur astronomers who are interested in observing asteroids from their own telescopes.

NASA Ask a Space Scientist
http://image.gsfc.nasa.gov/poetry/ask/askmag.html#list
Take a look at the Interactive Page where NASA scientists answer your questions about astronomy, space, and space missions. This site also has access to archives and fact sheets.

NASA Newsroom
http://www.nasa.gov/newsinfo/newsroom.html
This site features NASA's latest press releases, status reports, and fact sheets. It includes a news archive with past reports and a search button

for the NASA website. You can even sign up for e-mail versions of all NASA press releases.

National Space Society
600 Pennsylvania Avenue, S.E., Suite 201
Washington, DC 20003
http://www.nss.org

The Nine Planets: A Multimedia Tour of the Solar System
http://www.seds.org/nineplanets/nineplanets/nineplanets.html
This site has excellent material on moons. It was created and is maintained by the Students for the Exploration and Development of Space, University of Arizona.

Planetary Missions
http://nssdc.gsfc.nasa.gov/planetary/projects.html
At this site, you'll find NASA links to current and past missions. It's a one-stop shopping center to a wealth of information.

The Planetary Society
65 North Catalina Avenue
Pasadena, CA 91106-2301
http://www.planetary.org/

Terrestrial Impact Craters
http://spaceart.com/solar
Information on impact craters, including educators' notes.

Windows to the Universe
http://windows.ivv.nasa.gov/
This NASA site, developed by the University of Michigan, includes sections on "Our Planet," "Our Solar System," "Space Missions," and "Kids' Space." Choose from presentation levels of beginner, intermediate, or advanced. To begin exploring, go to the URL and choose "Enter the Site."

Places to Visit

Check the Internet (*www.skypub.com* is a good place to start), your local visitor's center, or phone directory for planetariums and science museums near you. Here are a few suggestions.

American Museum of Natural History
West 79th Street and Central Park West
New York, NY
http://www.amnh.org/
The largest collection of meteorites in existence is on display here.

Exploratorium
3601 Lyon Street
San Francisco, CA 94123
http://www.exploratorium.edu
You'll find internationally acclaimed interactive science exhibits, including astronomy subjects.

Jet Propulsion Laboratory (JPL)
4800 Oak Grove Drive
Pasadena, CA 91109
http://www.jpl.nasa.gov/faq/#tour
JPL is the primary mission center for all NASA planetary missions. Tours are available once or twice a week by arrangement.

Meteor Crater
Meteor Crater Enterprises, Inc.
P.O. Box 70
Flagstaff, AZ 86002-0070
http://www.meteorcrater.com/
http://www.barringercrater.com
Site in Arizona where a large iron-nickel asteroid plummeted into Earth's crust 50,000 years ago, producing a crater that is nearly a mile wide. A visitor's center and Museum of Astrogeology recounts the history of the crater, and visitors can observe the crater from several observation sites along the rim.

NASA Goddard Spaceflight Center
Code 130, Public Affairs Office
Greenbelt, MD 20771
http://pao.gsfc.nasa.gov/vc/info/info.htm
Visitors can see a Moon rock brought back to Earth by Apollo astronauts as well as other related exhibits.

National Air and Space Museum
7th and Independence Ave., S.W.
Washington, DC 20560
http://www.nasm.edu/
This museum, located on the National Mall west of the Capitol building, has all kinds of interesting exhibits.

Space Center Houston
Space Center Houston Information
1601 NASA Road 1
Houston, Texas 77058
Space Center Houston offers a tour and exhibits related to humans in space, including the Apollo missions to the Moon.

Bold numbers indicate illustrations.

Ray Spangenburg and **Kit Moser** are a husband-and-wife writing team specializing in science and technology. They have written 33 books and more than 100 articles, including a 5-book series on the history of science and a 4-book series on the history of space exploration. As journalists, they covered NASA and related science activities for many years. They have flown on NASA's Kuiper Airborne Observatory, covered stories at the Deep Space Network in the Mojave Desert and experienced zero-gravity on NASA experimental flights out of the NASA Ames Space Center. They live in Carmichael, California, with their two dogs—Mencken (a Sharpei mix) and F. Scott Fitz (a Boston terrier).

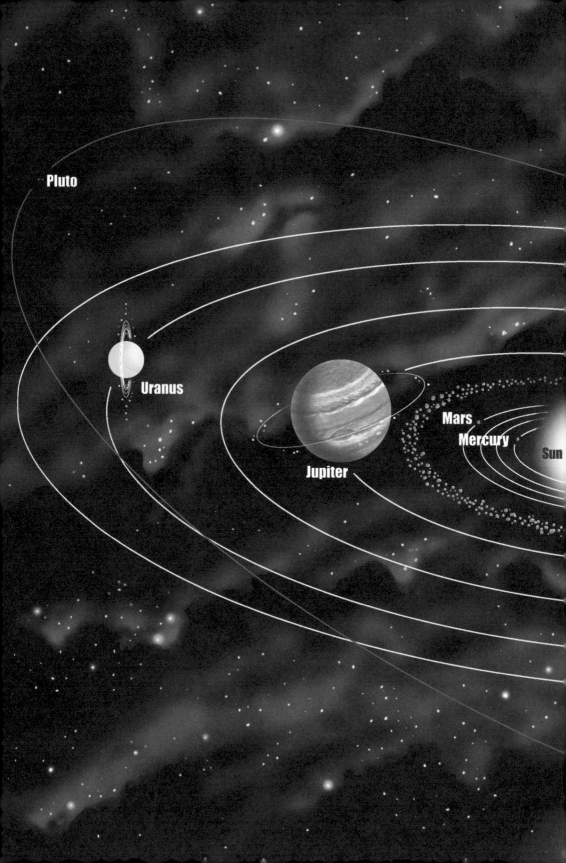